TRESPASSERS WELCOME

Poems by

Kathy Evans

BLUE LIGHT PRESS ◆ 1ST WORLD PUBLISHING

1ST WORLD
PUBLISHING

SAN FRANCISCO ◆ FAIRFIELD ◆ DELHI

BLUE LIGHT PRESS
www.bluelightpress.com
bluelightpress@aol.com

1ST WORLD PUBLISHING
PO Box 2211
Fairfield, IA 52556
www.1stworldpublishing.com

BOOK & COVER DESIGN
Melanie Gendron
melaniegendron999@gmail.com

COVER ART
Liana Steinmetz

AUTHOR PHOTO
Sean Evans

FIRST EDITION

Library of Congress Control Number: 2019956404

ISBN: 978-1-4218-3644-7

ACKNOWLEDGMENTS

I would like to thank my family and friends, particularly those who offered their support in shaping this book:

Molly Giles, Tom Centolella, Linda Wolfe, Giovanni Singleton, Elinor Gale, Barbara Holmes, Sean Evans, Riki Eastmond, Diane Frank, and so many others for their encouragement and musings: Dorianne Laux, Susy Stewart, Katharine Harer, Johnny Bondage, Sally Doyle, Jane Hirshfield, Scott and Ruffles Bennion, Ruthanne Martin, and the writing group, Jackie Kuddler, Barbara Brauer, and Doreen Stock. Special thanks to Liana Steinmetz for the cover art.

With added thanks to the editors of previous publications where these poems first appeared:

"Psychic Healers" published in *The Southern Review*
"Juvenile Hall" published in *Americas Review*
"A Normal Birth" published in *Runes*
"Crossing the Line" published in *The West Marin Review*
"I Am Letting You In" published in *Tupelo Press*

TABLE OF CONTENTS

III.

Found Poem in National Geographic

IV.

Found Poem on My Desktop

I.
Trespassers Welcome

(Found Poem on a Fence Post)

NOTE WRITTEN ON A NAPKIN

for Aly

Every year the irises appear,
a green straight elegance
with dark assertive tips.

Even when the fog settles,
I love how overnight
a single bud

will open
to what light there is,
how, with some reluctance, it is
drawn to its edges

the way you are drawn,
the way all desire
declares itself.

I GO TO JANE'S HOUSE TO WRITE

One hour at Jane's house
and I'm already into the ice cream, vanilla bean,
and I spill a bag of Columbian decaf from Peet's all over the freezer.
My eyes shuttle from shelf to sink to refrigerator —
an old Maytag with an adjust-temp.
Her refrigerator door is compelling.
A postcard of Einstein with his legs crossed,
a photo of her old dog, Maggie. The poets
held under circular magnets, Czeslaw Milosz, Robert Frost,
a $15 dollar off coupon —
Seamus Heaney with his sly smile, squinty eyes,
and beautiful bushy eyebrows — what a constellation.
This from Stanley Kunitz, "At every stage in life we need
to create a self that we can bear to live and die with."
Now that seems like good advice.
That's why I've come to Jane's house — to find a new self,
a more disciplined self, one who will write everyday,
instead of the one who looks at the beauty magazines
and eats ice cream. I'll get used to the red clock,
its measured ticks. I'll come to love the blue pilot light,
its steady flame. Jane has salt. Jane is salt. She has a Cuisinart
and daffodils in a clear vase placed on a simple wooden table.
If I can't write here, I can't write anywhere. She has
a microfiber mop and two umbrellas, one from Krakow.
She has Wellies for the winter rain and sandals —
I swear from the Seventies — for the summer, tiny metal frogs
under her candle holders.
And to think she has entrusted all this to me.
I haven't even made it past the kitchen —
with its hard honey in a bear pot,
herbs of Provence, and chopped sea clams.
Her good knives in the rack pointing straight down,

and her asparagus pointing straight up —
like the green horns of the devil.
But no devils here, no sireee, not in this house, just uplifting
botanicals and excellent books in hardback. The garden,
just beyond the kitchen window in all its regalia.
It calls me to the pebbled path; out to the lavender
and camellias; to the magnolia,
opening its plate size blossoms of white
against the green leaves; out to the apple trees almost in bloom.
"They bloom last," she said, as she left through the gate.
"Just look at these bearded irises. Remember all you do is
water and weed," she paused, pulling her Samsonite
down the driveway, "and, of course, write."

A NORMAL BIRTH

you make yourself on the inside of
me   little   goblin   god-
one   swim   beige   being
in brine and borrow yourself some   blood
and take all the   cells   you'll need
    while you gaze through your
slipper gauze   your galaxy of bones
                  just below
my xylophone   a whole marimba band you   famished
little embryo   building a dome
    in the plaza plasma   ten-fingered   radiant
light-weight champion
    a   foot here   and   an ardent protrusion
fist-popping there   in the tub   in the inner-world scribble
on me   from the inside
    while I walk around with us both on   the outside
your muscled moments   upside down
    in my cytoplasmic casaba cabana cabin   like
those weightless ones in space —

        a boy/girl tremble   taut
            taking me out   out   out   on the town
        in my tents   Birth   is just   a change
in tense   you'll see,   you little   high C
slide right out   and give me back my waist
you little   thief   thump
but not without some pain,
        forceps   and   a forward
                              plop
a little umph, a rumba and a   thrust
breathebreathebreathe

a right or left
Punch and Judy me   counting down to three
   breathe   heave ho   and there

you little astronaut still tethered to the mother ship
   goat milk blue   and no longer
cohering —   Look!   we are
the new float in the Rose Bowl Parade
   give me your merry-
go-round ticket and I'll tear it in two   now   that
we are two divided by   one
      spank ah!   you —
a diagonal in air
   and I   in   my
            animal blood

THESE BOOKS

I love my books, even the ones that aren't mine, the ones
I have failed to return, Gretchen's *The Trespasser*, Tom's *Equus*,
and the other books sleeping like
orphans, toppling from shelves in heaps. Strunk and White
on top of *Women Approaching Menopause*. Here, missing for years,
is Chekhov, my sleek orange thrift edition.
I have read *all* of some of them, and *some* of all of them.
I have underlined and inked their margins,
trusting to my Parnassus of authors praise and blurb.
They, with their discipline
and dedication to thought, insight, reveries,
subtleties, epiphanies, the nailed down facts
and floating fictions, the characters who with *Iron Shoes*
compel us to follow them into the woods to the last page —
how their words move filaments against
the silken mysteries of light, sometimes
with raindrops held suspended along
the strands. I praise them, their linguistic musings,
their patient assembling, their sentences standing up.
Here, *The History of God* right next to *One Hundred Years of Solitude*,
Women in Their Beds next to *The Heart of Darkness*,
written, by god, well, by Conrad, no less, in his third language,
Simone De Beauvoir and Melville
placed on top of each other.
Rumi leaning into *Mrs. Dalloway*.
My apologies to *Ulysses*,
which I have not read, except in parts,
as well as *The Tibetan Book of the Dead*,
and my former debate partner's thesis —
The History of Grain Elevators.
I admit I'm a bit lazy.
But, listen, sometimes

in the deep womb of night
when one cannot sleep, and the great questions loom
larger than their insufficient answers,
I click off the remote
then pile my books near me, believing
that just as a tree makes chlorophyll,
these books and all their words
will enter beautifully through
my eyelids, into my slumbering sea lion body,
my cerebral cortex, my amygdala,
and I will awaken in the morning
well-read, sated, and wise.

AWESOME

The poet reading at the First Unitarian Church on Franklin,
spoke about plastic flowers and a street in Berkeley, and then said,
"Awesome!" I was shocked. Even he, a poet,
a man of words. Come on — *Awesome?*

The other day I overheard someone say, *Super Awesome.*
The word has galumphed into our overused everyday.
But, really, I mean Moses at the burning bush could have said,
Awesome! Buddha, after he removed the serpent from his eyes
and no longer felt fear — and the Bodhi tree? *Awesome.*
Tibet and the tallest mountain, the roof of the world.
My lord, Jesus just walked on the water! *Awesome!*
The Goldberg Variations, slot canyons around Escalante, Utah,
jellyfish. But a poem about plastic pink flowers
and a side street in Berkeley?

Once a few years back, at the International School in Salt Lake City,
I was asked by a Brazilian student in my ESL class,
What is Awesome? "O que es awesome?"
They spoke Portuguese; I didn't. Not a word.
Everyone was saying Awesome in Utah, especially the teenagers.
I pointed to the snowy peaks of the Rocky Mountains
right out beyond the window. I went down on my knees,
then lifted my arms in the air, and said, *Awesome.* But no one
really got it because everyone said Awesome for everything including
scrambled eggs and bacon,
which I guess if you think about it on a plate
how the bacon got there and the eggs, it is awesome —
the butchering ritual of a pig, the chicken laying
an egg in the dimly lit coop. The birth of anything, really!

Then one morning for a field trip, our class walked down
to the new library, designed by
the notable Egyptian architect, Moshie Safdie.
And after walking all the way down in the snow —
they being from Brazil, of course, a little underdressed,
one girl in very sexy cut offs —
we were huddled inside in the entry, standing under
a magnificent skylight, and looked high up. A delicate mobile
of small silver birds shimmered with the slightest movement
in the light. We could see clouds floating across
the geometric glass against the bluest sky. I lifted my arms
up again and said *Awesome!*
Awesome! they repeated.
One Brazilian kid slapped the other Brazilian kid, five!

Later that night after the poetry reading,
making our way home in the car,
Giovanni said that if she had kids
their names would be Thurgood and Ocean.
I looked at her and said, *Awesome!*

CROSSING THE LINE

Listening to Credence Clearwater right outside of Mesquite,
it's barely green here, but Cedar Pocket is just up ahead.
The bluffs and buttes rising up in big slabs of time —
the fingerings, the riffs. Maybe life is just the next
three miles up with a lingering song on the radio,
a signal still within reach.
The clouds seem painted on, so floaty and beautiful.
Where Would You Be Without Love,
sing the Doobie Brothers. All I know
is I am behind a truck called the Earth Roamer,
an XVLT, headed straight to the Virgin River
where the water runs mud red to a trickle.
Heat shimmies in waves. The soaring Broadwings
fly in on cue. There's an old pick-up and a port of entry,
but you can't pull in until the lights are flashing.
I've crossed the corners of three states
and not a model home yet, not a single suburb —
the mind traveling toward the next rest stop
with its blue *No Services* sign — just distance and desert
where it is safe to go into time alone
with Fleetwood Mac and the gypsy. *Lightning once, maybe twice —*
or a good place for the stone dead.
Pleased to meet you
Hope you guess my name.

NOE AND SIMONE

When the second baby came,
Noelle, the big sister, two and a half,
became a small Godzilla.
No kidding, not out of jealously exactly,
or envy, not
out of sibling rivalry or a kind of
primate displacement, as we had expected,
but something more primitive,
more fierce — the two P's,
Possession and Protection.
She took her role as the big sister,
not unlike some governments, very seriously,
shaking the cage,
stepping over bridges,
guarding the sister city
at any cost.
She became the Nightmare on Bryant Street,
stomping down the hall if anyone
came near, thrashing about,
guarding the door in her polka dot rain boots.
At first Noe thought her new sister
was a doll that just moved,
and when she discovered that the
baby sister was real,
it was her job to keep her little sister
safe. She would throw herself
on the ground to prevent
passage into the nursery, guard
the bedroom door with a plastic plate
and sword, snatch
toys from the pudgy hands
of small cousins who posed any

immediate threat, then run
down the hall into the room
and throw in her small collection
of ammunition — sippy cups,
rubber ducks, stuffed bears,
pacifiers, alphabet blocks.
Wham! Into the Pack & Play,
into the crib. She'd raise her arms
and go off like a blaring police alarm.
"My Baby Sister," she'd yell,
then follow it with "MINE!"
We were a little worried as citizens
of the house. It was a kind of
beautiful ferocity we had never
witnessed. And each morning
when she awoke, she would ask,
"Is my sister still here?"
We, her subjects, her villagers,
her slaves and serfs
in the kingdom
of early childhood would nod,
bleary-eyed, "yes!"
as she went hunting,
passing through each door, possessed,
looking for her baby sister,
her tiny, quiet sister,
sleeping inside a blanket
like a rose petal.
Her sweet baby sister
Simone!

JUVENILE HALL

Today in Juvy, Marcel says
he's gonna' sing his poem,
that two weeks ago he didn't even know
what a poem was, that it just came out.
"It just came out," he says,
"like a baby comes out of a woman."
That's what he says,
as if he knows.
He says he's never even written a poem before,
but this one just wants to be sung,
and he smiles crooked-like, looks
charmingly cockeyed,
places his arms on the classroom podium.
"Now, I know you're gonna' want to laugh
when I sing my poem
and I'll just ask you brothers to wait,
to hold your laugh until I'm done.
I'm just sayin' wait."
And the big boys at the back
in their faded orange t-shirts and dark sweats,
with their shaved heads and sneers, some with
cheek scars from a quick knife, or pierced lips —
the boys from Richmond, from the hood,
some with biceps that seemed bolted on,
they just stared at Marcel,
while he filled his lungs and sang
about his girl who had the baby anyway,
and his baby girl,
how she just came out like a poem —
that sweet baby girl, how they'd made it
together, then lost it.
Sang until the brothers in the back wanted to sing, too.

Seriously, joined in at the end.
I swear the whole class up at Juvy was stunned
when Marcel was done with his poem —
the guards by the door, the boys at the back,
the parole officer in blue,
the nurse who dispenses pale pills in Dixie cups,
and the poetry teacher, who was all of a sudden
just one of them, one with them, one with Marcel
and the brothers up in Juvy because sometimes a poem
just wants to be sung.

II.

Can the Dead Speak?

Are Virgin Mary Sightings Real?

Call for a Free Book.

(Found Poem on a billboard outside Walgreens)

ON THE FRONT PAGE OF THE NEW YORK TIMES —
A PHOTOGRAPH

Children dressed in colored parkas and pink
and purple backpacks walk through the snow toward
a school bus in Little Silver, New Jersey.
Snowflakes sift over them, as if to say
they are safe inside a snow globe.

In the lower left hand corner of the page
a man in blue ear muffs on a small snow cat
shovels snow toward the U. S. with its
stiff demands for weapons of mass destruction.
Shoveling under the Catholic Diocese
bracing for a new swift lawsuit,
shoveling toward the drug traffickers laundering millions
out of Mexico, moving away from the West Bank,
turning over Bethlehem, uprooting Syria,
heading toward air bases in Turkey.

Meanwhile, the children wear boots that squeak
in freshly fallen snow.
We drink coffee in America. Outside in the mall
sparrows gather in bare winter trees.
It's the end of Chanukah.
In one week, it will be Christmas.

It's as if right now
we have pressed the pause button
while the bundled children
walk though the snow toward a school bus
because school has been let out early
in Little Silver, New Jersey.

DIALOGUE WITH THE INVISIBLE

The poet, Lew Welch, vanished with no trace.
The stones in the creek won't.
The fish might. The water might.

Bride of fences, birds of paradise —
  all yesterday yards of sunlight.

Sometimes it's too much to take in.
Then we'll do take-out.
It takes it out of us — don't you think?

Don't say us.
One person, one flat screen, a televised tsunami,
an oil spill, a shootout, an Arab Spring, a beheading,
Bahrain, a deadly marathon, a new Pope,
a bad election, a travesty, poverty, a royal wedding,
a wall, AK47s, Syria —
serious fundamental stuff here.
Gaza. Heat.
Run, for god's sake. Run.
Don't say god — survival then. Run.

Just think about it.
The Dark Knight — birds off course in the wind turbines.
I know the bees, the reefs. How many tigers?

Let's go back to pale and luscious peonies,
the folds of pink that shield the explosive center.

A casual elegy, an
elegiac casualty.
Our world littered with heat and bits.
Cut and memory, and no one is paying attention.

Birds on the long end of the wind.
God is soft.
Don't say ours.
It equates.
Hard information then — hard facts.
Beauty, after all, after all, is just an addendum.
I miss touching.
Don't say I. Then what?
Maps and apps. Text me.
The night is an immigrant.
We're still here.
Frond, fraud, fraught with —
The loud page with its legs open.
Everything happens
in the blink of an i pad —
Stay in your cell.

God, the circuit or the circuit breaker?
Oh, these little hours of ours.
Don't say ours—

The big God reported to be above the whales,
the little god inside the sea shell.
Club sandwiches and white people —

things get tagged —
substance, subversive, spam,
a shuttle between subject and object.
Where did the predicate go? It is all so unpredictable.
Think about it —
those horses on the cave walls, the glyphs.
Tell me it's all a matter of time.
I'll tell you it is so quiet at the end of the paragraph,
it's like a nurse's cap.
Some people believe in reincarnation.

They go to Colorado to stand in front of antennas,
or Egypt to the pyramids to ask the questions.

We tag dead things. *Don't say we.*

It is always the self on self with or without the narrative.
Well, the bees, remember?

It's flotsam. Figure it out.
Do you mean me?
Don't say me.
Saints don't. They grow herbs and are perhaps better
at kneeling with the goats in the bluebells.

He gave her a look.
She was so beat she left to pet the dog.
The dog didn't flinch.

Sex — he could change out of his body afterwards
as if nothing happened.
She couldn't get rid of the scent for days,
and in an instant found out
she could still cry.
Cartographers and new fingers for Nietzsche.

Sing clouds first
then tell me about suffering —
Don't say me.

You're invited to stay over.
Stay.

ISMS

Because isms are dangerous
because isms are base camps
because isms collect eye glasses
throw lassos around free radicals
because isms bloat
blurt out
hurt
hunt
or swallow thoughts whole
to make a collective
because isms can't distinguish nuance
with isms there is only one window
seemingly sturdy but with an uncertain frame —
one angle, one porch, one patch of earth
because isms march
because isms blur the alternatives and the truth
because they blend into single entities
because isms sometimes bleed and
isms are schisms for propelling the movement
because I'm tired
because thinking things through thoroughly
takes too long
because isms grow barnacles
because isms grow gas chambers and trains
that only go one way.

NIGHT

I could not
name
the silence

it was a hidden
instrument
      in the reeds
a hushed storm
        outside
my blood that refused
      the noise

Once I could startle you
      rinse you clean
follow
      what had been
          erased —

There were parts of you
      only you knew
and places you didn't
   know at all
Your body became
      a tapestry of my thoughts —
Mine, a folded map in your hands

THE VIRGIN RIVER

When she walked into that river,
swam dog-like against the current,
she knew she was no virgin.
Look what water has done without memory.

Below canyon walls,
between vertical slabs of sandstone and shale,
she was a solitary figure
in a Chinese brush painting

as if she was being called by the river
toward a small slit of light
where the Narrows snap shut
like a book, as if

she was being scraped
against the thigh bones of an enormous woman,
pulled back into a fathomless entry,
and it was the way she glided belly down
toward death or birth that made her seem
so elegantly primitive.

SWITCH

My mother walks the underground garage
in a negligee.
Which key is which?
Which switch is which?

The phone rings. They want to know
if we want to switch.
Mother, it doesn't have to be all or nothing.
But it does.
She's letting go of whole sentences,
hanging onto sign language and phantoms,
tax deductions and the King of Thebes.

Who kneels there before me? A second self,
A mother? A belief system?
There is a new set of contradictions.
Follow me, she says.
And I do —
the faint scent
of lavender,
a ladder without rungs
we both climb.

A DREAM ABOUT MY MOTHER

I fell back asleep
and dreamed again about my mother,
the earlier mother. We
were sitting around the pool.
"Here," she said. "Give me the keys.
I'll drive."
Just like that. So
I lifted her up from the grass and carried her
over the patio
and held her by the shoulders.
She tried to straighten up, my rag doll mother,
took baby steps.
As we cut the corner
of the swimming pool, she fell in.
The aqua covered her, just like that, and I couldn't tell
if she was laughing or drowning,
trying so hard, so I jumped in after her and
saved my mother for another day,
and we swam like we used to
in the old pool
with our street clothes on, all the way to the deep end
and back.

QUIET
for Jake

so quiet
the prayer is quiet

quiet enough to hear
hair grow

the voice of ice

the tea bag

so quiet music notes rest
at rest stops

quiet enough for tumors
to stop growing

as quiet as snow falling
into
snow

as quiet as the inside

of a hat

EARLY SPRING

My mother will die in the Spring
when the snow is still on the ground
and the bright forsythia fans out
against the hospital bricks,
when saplings float a few white blossoms
over hard earth,
not unlike my
mother.

DAY OF THE DEAD

The day is perfectly November,
fog on the ridge, you can still see the mountain.
This weathered wooden deck still holding
the glass table with a seasonal pumpkin in the center.
All the people inside the cell phone have been silenced.
Digitals show up on the menu bar — a small regiment in black,
waving for the sake of time, the flag of surrender.
The weeds are higher than the windows, but this isn't my lot.
Remember Lot's wife —
when she looked back defiantly or unwittingly,
and turned to salt? Tonight I will be her,
sprinkle salt like breadcrumbs. What I'm trying to say is this:
We don't always find our way back
and the place is never the same anyway.
We need to know more witches, but instead
we go into therapy. Now is the time to love the dark center
of the sunflower, the hollowed-out skull,
spiders resting like eyes inside their webs. I personally
love the color of crows. Tonight I will walk with Tito
and the skeletons through the streets.
The dead will be among us.
We will remember our mothers,
their smell, their loose skin, and stroll with them
toward the bright altars of paper flowers
and the lit-up tamale trucks in the Mission.

THE BIG BAD WOLF

After reading Little Red Riding Hood to my granddaughter,
she asked me if the Big Bad Wolf lived in her neighborhood.
"No," I said, "the wolf lives in the forest not in the Mission district."
She looked at me and then the pictures
for a closer inspection.
After all, the wolf dressed up like the grandmother.
Then I thought about her question and the man
who sits on her stoop every Friday after the methadone clinic,
someone she calls her "homeless man"
and trustingly knows his name, Ned.
No wolf, just someone who needs a hand up.
And the other one, who shouts in the streets, who twice
defecated right outside the front door on the apartment step
because he was angry at the landlord
for yelling at him, calling him *pig* and *vermin* —
No, he is not a wolf either, just a man
in a rage outside the safety net. And what of the addicts sitting
on the curb in a park outside the church?
She once offered them a banana,
and one of them looked at the others and said, "Put the needles away.
There is a child here." Wolves? No, just addicts.
And then I remembered the two people,
slovenly and inebriated, who followed us
with a sloppy gait up lower 24th Street, and when
my granddaughter ran ahead of me and yelled,
"You can't catch me," one of them warned,
"Listen, lady, keep your eye on that one,
or she'll be snatched." So now I hold her hand tighter
at the light. I think of the forest, the pungent scent
of wolf and fallen leaves, the gnarled oaks,
and the path leading in, how the path
hardens and narrows in the dark
and then just
ends.

SWIMMING WITH DOREEN

I once lived heedless.
I was swimming then
not measuring my laps,
flying and dying
going in place of others
into radiant pinholes.
I was floating between layers
because I had found no one else to love.

Then, while staring at the goats in Mendocino,
I remembered a grammar school
in sunlight, suspended in amethyst and gold swirls,
an oasis of a kind
in early morning
like a high Galilee city.

To start over with desire,
I had to erase oblivion.
Into the sky flew a white bird
with my eyes, and I knew myself again.

ON THE HIGHWAY TO SPRING

the road buckled
      the crocus hadn't opened yet
          I fell into
           a long
              afternoon of
                  sky algebra
                      tree music
                          and dark

THE TRINITIES

early Easter morning

the Dogwood

in a light rain

along this narrow

mountain road

has also risen

ARCADE

When the Ferris wheel spun
and the pinball machine pinged,
she knew
the lit up angel
in the arcade
with one black wing
and a muscular arm was there.
It spoke to her and kept her steady
while she threw darts at the red
balloons, recalling
how she'd once been a boy.

WHAT THE FIFTH GRADERS SAID

They were telling me their dreams,
sitting at their desks, as if in translation.
The words began to fill the room.
We could hear the other children out on the playground —
their muffled squeals through the walls,
kick ball sounds and rolling carts.
Then words began to appear on the walls.
I began writing them down —
coyote, skull shadow, closet door. One child said
he had a dream that the numbers were too high.
It was a math dream.
Another told of a seizure he had in the hospital
where he dreamed he was falling into a lake of needles.
The girl with braids at the back said her father
was filling a rock canyon with liquid cement.
"What's her name?" Dottie spoke up.
"Sometimes I feel trapped like I'm in a small box,
never to be let out, and I grow younger."
Then the child from Iraq, I think his name was Sebri,
said that in real life, before he was born,
his dad was shot six times and lived.
"And now I dream my dad and I are on a carpet.
He picks me up in his arms, but he is a skeleton,
then I become one, too." At this point,
I feel it is my responsibility to take us in another direction.
I remember a dream that I had once under a tree
of pretty colors. A big rescue dog picked me up
with his mouth and slobbery jowls
and carried me into a magnificent meadow.
"There," I say, "there."

SPACES

for Hana

an eight year old child falls
                  through the air
    keeps falling through grass blades,
the s p a c e s between slot canyons,
        middle c   and   b flat,
            the blanks between rain
    and haikus,
wasps and dark holes —
    she is a blown feather
further up
        drifting
           above her mother's hair,
her father's shoulders,
        into and through
her sister's hands,
    she is between sand and sand,
      stars and black holes
between   there   and   then,
  and then not there —
    she remains in the air
  an ellipsis,
for a long time
           after-
wards

BYE-BYE EVELYN

Damn! If the ice cream man don't show up
in his jingle truck
just in time for the noon day ball.
We'll line-dance in the ripples,
Move our hips to the continental shift.
Tap shoes and step ball change, hot
tar and slide guitar —
You're such a little wiggle worm.
We say shiny dimes and chocolate.
We say you're my little peach
blossom. We say yum —
bees darting like little B-52s into
the very center of the flutter
while the ruby-throated hummingbird
leads us smack down to the end of the
cul de sac. Love is this and that. But mostly this.
We say damn! That's punctual.
Please, nothing genetically engineered.
Feliz Navidad. We say hot rum and tinsel.
We'll take both — silk purse and sow's ear.
Spumoni and Jesus Christ, hot fudge
and jubilee. We say good luck next time,
make an offering to the life force. We say
you crack me up.

III.

The Meercats of Australia
swallow the stingers of scorpions
and then spit them out satisfied!

(*Found Poem in National Geographic*)

SUMMONS

In the house on the avenues
we'd arrive slippered
or barefoot in the cold hall,
pulled, not by steamed windows, nor
the sudden light on the snow outside;

not by the work shirt over the back of a chair,
the soft wallet and the keys,

but by the smell —

the coffee,
finding its way up the stairs —
a kind of temptress,
or a religious call.

And we'd follow it pure from
sleep, where she'd be there each time —

our mother,

pouring
the first black cup.

TERRITORY

I climb Horse Hill with a bucket of pears —
one each for the roan gelding with its satin fetlock,
silk haunch, and swoosh of tail — the Morgan and mares,
all of them with such handsome manes.
They grace the hills above the freeway, graze,
and in the early morning, sometimes you can see them
take off at full gallop across the ridge. The suburb
has saved this hill for them,
taken it back from the developers on bulldozers.

A rainbow appears.
How many rainbows appear simultaneously over the earth?
Do they hang above slaughterhouses?
Above mass graves, above terrorists?
Do terrorists call themselves terrorists?
A horse pulls from my hand the flesh of pear, snorts,
then those big horse teeth.
The cars below tell their own story at rush hour.
Someone looks up from the car pool lane.
We love territory.
We die for it.

THE PAINT DREAM

Last night I dreamed Trump came onto me.
Me too, of all women. I mean, I'm seventy-two.
I was painting walls in the White House,
all speckled in my paint clothes.
He was in a tux wearing his red
Make America Great Again hat, which he offered me.
"No, I like my paint hat," I told him emphatically, "and my
coveralls!" The walls were a ghastly green,
a sludgy swamp green, with little gold flecks. Nothing
was getting covered up completely with my roller because
the walls were all embossed from the Jackie Kennedy re-do days.
No one had a clue. The white was showing through.
I remembered Mrs. White did it in the dining hall
with the revolver.
Trump, with his puff hair, kept at it; he was like a bouncer.
I was looking for a way out,
maybe through the servants' entry.
If there was just some way to get to the rose garden.
I went through a door, and there I was
in the press room with Sarah Huckabee Sanders, her hair
darker and stringier than I'd remembered. She looked Amish.
She was choked up, genuinely so this time, because a little boy
representing *Time Magazine For Kids* was asking her questions
about the NRA and why doesn't President Trump... and because
she has a child too, she almost started to cry in that room
of the disingenuous. I had a few questions for her, but
Stormy Daniels was in the room and I did not
have a chance in hell, which is where I think I was.
Trump came in and stood behind me. Maybe he thought
I was Russian. That was it. I jabbed him with my paint roller,
ruining his tux. I just needed an exit through the right door.
No, not the right door and not the left door, just a door door.

We all do. I jabbed him once again, and said,
"Go Away. Shoo fly, don't bother me.
Mrs. White did it in the Library with the gun!"
The Secret Service grabbed me, dragged me through a tunnel.
"This needs a little paint, too." I said.
"Take your hands off me. I'm just a common citizen.
Get back in there now," I yelled, "and make America
safe again!" and they released me and that was that.
I crossed the border.

ECLIPSE

Tucson — August.
Everyone in the house is awake at 4 a.m.
The ceiling fan on high in the Tucson heat,
so hot you can barely breathe;
the two-year-old in the green-gray crib is left to cry it out
through its own lungs and a two alarm nightmare;
the mommy in the hall jiggling the new baby close
to her body in the Ergo; the daddy
"sofaed-out" on t.v. — Season 3, Episode 10;
the matriarch wide-awake under the whirling fan,
watching her digital watch. A new house on a quiet street,
freshly painted in taupe and cream and cactus green,
all new appliances; on the roof, a disabled air-conditioner
the size of a small space station. And because
there is no screen time allowed on any of the devices,
no newspaper, no radio, they don't know what's coming —
the locusts, the dark web, the neo-Nazis, the oligarchs;
nor that climate change is right outside the French doors
in 115 degree Fahrenheit black heat; no one knows the floods
are coming, the long-range missiles, the fires in paradise,
nor that tomorrow there will be an eclipse.
Alexa, play
If You're Happy and You Know It . . .

ECLIPSE 2

According to NASA,
an eclipse is a celestial
coincidence.
Early surfers
are out there
right now
with super lenses,
trying to catch the first ominous
moon shadow falling
like ash
over
the Western
shore. There are
people waiting
for little moons to collapse onto
the shaded earth, for the path
of totality with its eerie dark
to show them
the way.

PSYCHIC HEALERS

I never liked the anteroom of my analyst's office,
all those East Indian relics against beige, an
ashtray from Harrah's in Reno, swag light
on dim, and piles of old *New Yorkers,*
which I flipped through furtively for the captions
under the cartoons, for any kind of humor, actually.
The quiet was palpable, and I could feel the weight
of the San Francisco fog lean against her office door.
Once she fell asleep in a session. I did not
wake her. Compliant, complacent, I allowed her to dream her own
Jungian dreams — dark men in five o'clock shadow, a red hibiscus
opening, anima, animus. I merely
sat there and studied the bones
in her wrists, yammered rhythmically on and on,
mantra-like, about sex, death, and my pathological
tardiness. The Navajo rug as a backdrop, her cocked head
could have been the perfect
Andrew Wyeth — Helga lines around the eyes.
When she woke, I did not mention that she'd dozed,
nor for how long, because of — you know — the transference-
counter-transference thing. I merely said at the end
of the session, "My dead father stands
each night at the foot of my bed. Everyday I walk through
a different Bay Area shopping mall in a tennis skirt.
I hate summer. Things die. And just last week,
I put my sleeping infant on a cot inside a display tent
at Big Five and left her there. Am I having a nervous breakdown?"
"No," she said, standing dim and fatigued
next to her shelf collection of cactus and succulents.
"You are experiencing what we call a
'personality disintegration.'"
"Oh," I said, "I feel so much better!

And what do you advise?"
"Be good to yourself," she offered.
"Take a friend to lunch, long walks to the beach,
hot baths, and go to a good Chinese restaurant." So I did.
That hour. I walked back to my car, and drove along
the panhandle of the park, along the boulevard
of churches, down into the Tenderloin, past Macy's
and the flower carts on the corners of Union Square,
down into the financial district. I parked the car
in a tow away zone, phoned Mary on the 16th floor
of the Transamerica Building, and while waiting for her
to descend, watched a stunt man scale the outside
of the pyramid, as if it were El Capitan. Mary emerged through the
double glass doors wearing a fabric of roses.
She looked like a Queen Anne chair,
and I needed to sit.
She insisted instead that we walk
through Chinatown. The walk would do me good. So we strolled
Grant Avenue past windows of whole chickens and cheap silks,
back alley smells of wet garbage,
fried won tons, and dim sum; tables of trinkets and souvenirs —
Chinese pajamas, carved elephant tusks,
flimsy flip-flops, until we
finally came to the restaurant.
"This is it," Mary said.
I half-expected an epiphany. We sank into the red vinyl
booth, unwrapped our chopsticks. I fingered the chrome napkin
holder. "Mary," I said, while staring down at the sweet and sour,
"I am experiencing a personality disintegration."
"A what?" she asked, cupping her tea. " Just shut up,
and open your fortune cookie." So I did. But nothing
was in it, not a single strip, and my purse was gone.
Mary picked up the tab,
and when we walked back to the car,
it was gone, too. I looked up. The gray sky was immense

The man on the outside on the building a mere speck.
After that day, I quit seeing my analyst.
Summer was summer, and her rates went up.
But two weeks later a man phoned to say
he'd found my purse. It had been left on a bench
in Washington Square. He was calling to return it.
Imagine! to return it!
So I drove into the city and stood on the corner
of Columbus and Broadway with a hand-scribbled sign
that read, *The Missing Purse Lady.* A man with a pink
face, a cherubic smile, and a bottle in his jacket
shuffled up and handed it over. Of course,
I expected everything to be gone, a sign of further
disintegration. Instead, when I unzipped my oversized
bag, everything was there — everything, and more —
white finger bowls, spoons, fireworks, rubber snakes,
Chinese slippers, a deck of cards, three watches,
and a jade snuff bottle. A shoplifter, a purse-snatcher,
crafty as hell, moving right up through Chinatown
with my purse! How propitious! I kissed the man,
handed him two of the watches, the snakes, the snuff
bottle, a full deck, and slapped down in his palm
the only twenty I had in the bag.
He smiled and slurred abundantly. We
embraced on Broadway. "Thank you,"
I said. "Thank you." The late afternoon sun bounced
off the windows of the distant office buildings.
Light fell over the pyramid. Someone switched on
the neon, and I felt fine, just fine.

ANGELS

for Sally

They can hang up colors we have never seen before
on days we rarely celebrate like Arbor Day.
Some appear without wings
or fake wings
pinned to the trapezius muscle,
no ropes to lift them from the ground.

I've seen bare-foot angels
with real hair on their toes
who don't levitate.

There was William Blake's angel
who wasn't nice at all, but fierce,
who hovered over the poet's bed
in broad daylight, and said
without fanfare, "Get up."

They don't always appear in forests, you know,
or in church knaves. Some like
a good coffee shop and cream pie,
or a bar where the bottles are lined up
in gleams of long light.

Most angels, can you believe it, avoid cemeteries
and crypts, unless they can take the shape of a bird.
I think pelicans over seawater are angels.
I do believe they love clouds, as we do, particularly
the alto-cumulus bunched up like soft bedding.

They also like a good bargain, a 75% off sale, where
they can trade in the white robe
for faux fur or a good wool coat,

which they give to someone on the street
who really feels the cold, as they continue up
a dark block to sing in the choir
where no one else has shown up for practice.

IV.

It's not you
it's your ad blocker.

(A Found Poem on my desktop)

MONTANA, SWAN RIVER

You enter the night
like a bather into a pond,
first your ankles, then your
knees. Waist high now —
Swim. Let the dark water
cover you.

Two deer in the high grass
move like shadows.
No moon.

Tomorrow
the hill will be softer
in colors of copper and rose.

Insects will erase themselves
as easily as you do.
You'll follow yourself back down
into the deepest part,

studying the imprints
left on the grass,
where they must have been warm
in their luminous sleep
and yours.

MT. TAMALPAIS

Fog slipping around
the base of the mountain,

the soft emergent green
of December.

Redwoods
drip
rain.

We're still here
in the air of birds.

OPTIMIST STICKERS

Today I can't decide. Should I buy a new witch hat
or the silver necklace with the tear drop
from the Little Shop of Hope?
I choose both. Lost my phone somewhere after the CT scan,
so I'm now just testing out my own personal data system, myself,
while offering prayers to whatever.
The homeless outside Mt. Zion are sitting on concrete piles
with their own piles — dark plastic bags
pillowed with stuff, squeezed
and bound with bright bungee cords. I feed the meter.
Buy. Rent. Borrow. The day has begun.
Men in coveralls ascending the scaffolding onto the glass above —
working class angels in hard hats.
It's already tomorrow in Melbourne, Australia,
and Rick, the parking lot attendant, tells me he knows everything
about the Rolling Stones. They've been around so long
he calls them the Rolling Bones, then hands me
a ripped off cd of Neil Young singing *Mother Earth*, which he
informs me was written for Neil's mother. Flowers growing on walls,
jackhammers tearing up the streets, optimist stickers
pasted on a storefront in English and Chinese.
I can't decide. Should I quit the Amoxicillin
because it gives me hives
and my lips double in size, or just let myself bloat
with the Prednisone like a Goodyear blimp and go up up
like a *Spirit in the Sky* with Norman Greenbaum, who hit it big

in 1969. A hippie dude. Just sayin',
or into *Time* with the Chambers Brothers?
Instead I decide to go for Jewish soup on 24th and Shotwell
to Wise & Sons, where they have homemade matzoh balls,
world famous babka, and Hetch Hetchy water.
Don't you just love the word delicatessen? Here
where the sign reads, *Sumptuous Dark Coffee* and
Eat Something. You look Skinny.
Plus the big red one over the door,
In America you can eat Challah every day.
Of course, unless you are homeless, or live in Charlottesville.
Remember Charlottesville? You should remember Charlottesville
because the country is getting cut up into big slabs of pie.
Inside by the cooler there are two
Chinese men in ball caps, tourists in white golf shirts,
a Hispanic gal with a Brooklyn accent,
and a soup line spooling in through the door.
Crazy Love is playing on the overhead.
I spy my granddaughter outside in the crosswalk in one of those
nursery school centipedes — children in little lime green t-shirts
holding onto a rope, crossing the intersection with their teacher —
I spot her legs in the rosebud tights.
"It's Nana," I yell from the doorway.
All the children turn and wave,
thinking I am their nana, too. That's what I'm talking about —
it's just a short distance from the Little Shop of Hope
to the delicatessen.

CHANGE OF ADDRESS

The last we heard
she was sleeping near a moose
in a single bed near the shore.
She could hear the waves flop onto the sand.
A large pink moon rose
over her like blown glass.
The house
had disappeared
but she hadn't.
And that was the lesson.

I AM LETTING YOU IN

on a big secret
On the third day of creation   eyes
Once before I was born I was   a hoof
 Music wasn't created yet, but   leaves were

Behind our perception of sky   another sky, darker
Colors had not been born
Language was the last fire   the first smoke

Who came up with numbers?   well, it wasn't God

We thought that pods and leaves and gold ran sideways

This could all exist in the imagination   I know is just a gigabyte

You tell me what came first   a kiss came first

Seeds can be deceptive
I didn't exist on the first day   I wasn't there yet
In the beginning was not a beginning   there was no beginning
only   a light
from the top of the darkness
something cracked
something spilled

THE KISS

The kiss wants us on both sides of it
like an equation.
It has said so.
And we want the kiss
to bind us, to fasten us, to keep us
steadfast. We want the kiss
to lie between us, make its way out of its bed
into ours in the dead of night.
We want to fall asleep kissing the kiss,
wake up to its mouth as well as our own,
and to each other's. We are its cave.
It sleeps in there sometimes,
and we are its water surrounding this island,
this kiss, this island, this kiss.
We are the body of water around it.
The kiss is molecular.
We are its particles,
the place that pulls between us
its own weight and mass.
The kiss is an erotic transaction, a low-key
metrical pattern that gives
structure and form. It is also medicinal,
centrifugal, and wet.
I watch its smallest movements
almost a pulse, pushing against
the breast of a finch. Our breath
pushes out this way. The kiss
has come on wings and bird's feet.
The throat knows the kiss. The intricate ear
asks for it, receives it. The tongue
and the mouth belong to the kiss.
They are its messengers.

We know the kiss will find us when we
are lost, bring us back to our bodies
with pragmatic rapture. We will
return from the kiss lighter.
It will return us to ourselves lighter.
The kiss will then rest between us,
a small sun sliding into
the Great Continental Divide.

TOTALLY

My grown daughter, when agreeing with someone
in conversation, will often end with "Totally."
I think such confirmation should be saved
for more cosmic events, say, a lunar cycle
where certain species have been known
to synchronize their breeding,

or a total solar eclipse where spiders,
like disgruntled campers, break down their webs,
hippos in Zimbabwe leave their rivers,
owl monkeys stop foraging,
a lunar eclipse when mass spawning in a coral reef
happens all at once and ten thousand eggs
released in the dark. Totally.

My granddaughter, on the other hand,
can put together complex puzzles totally fast.
Mind you, she is four.
The other night she put the entire United States of America
back together again in ten minutes — someone has to.
I reminded her, "Kansas is missing."
She said, "Well, look under the rug."
Her baby brother almost destroyed
the room next to us. He is the Tyrannosaur of the living room,
and we love him, totally.

Meanwhile, on this quiet street,
finally in a quiet corner of the living room,
I am in awe of the human brain, and how like a train,
it can switch tracks in the layered terminal,
part of the train on one track, part of it on another —
all those containers and compartments lined up,
even one with a sleeping berth.

I am totally in awe of squid ink,
and how orchids differentiate to become themselves.
And woodpeckers. What are they up to?
Pink flamingos how and why they stand on one leg,
tucking their crooked necks and streamlined heads
under one soft pink wing.

When I think of our lives orbiting out there in space
like raw data — pineapples growing out of the ground like small huts,
a snake slipping its skin, a blue agave,
meteors and eczema, toes, wings, cocoons,
our biological impulses and our political undoings,
I am astonished. Totally.

DEATH VALLEY

for Riki

just this —
rock wall
mudstone
sky

or this —
apricot mallow
ghost flower
mesquite

at night
under big stars
when we placed our hands and feet
in the eyeholes of the rock and
climbed skyward

everything large
and small
seemed to be
watching

THE HOUR

This is the hour the day has forgotten,
the hour where Black has its arms out
and the enormous sky wants in.
This is the hour Red gets quiet.
It's the grainy end of the day —
books fall open
and words wander near us
then away.
It is the thin color of nothing in a cup,
the hour of slippage and tenderness
when the horizontal dreamers float off,
and the technicians of midnight
begin.

DINNER PARTY

The invitations were sent out early.
Dinner, of course, was served in the cellar.
All guests were seated at one table — the living
and the dead. They ate by candlelight.
Shadows fell across the sand.
There was the scent of sandalwood, stewed meats
and cinnamon. A woman in a white blouse
and a midnight blue skirt brought hard loaves of bread
to the table, olives in small bowls.
No one talked of love or war,
only of the storm.
Caliban ate on one haunch near the fire. Ariel
blessed the wine. The living lifted their glasses;
the dead sprinkled salt.
Prospero poured, made a toast,
To the good dark, said he, *to next year,*
to nymphs, poetry, and chaste crowns,
to all we inherit,,
to all that must dissolve.

A DAY

I'll just start. I remember everything.
I asked you the name of a tree in your front yard
with leaves just turning a late August yellow.
I had driven miles down The Pacific Coast Highway to see you.
You said, "Dutch Elm." You said, "I have an idea,"
and handed me a spray bottle and a rag,
and we went into the greenhouse. Sunlight followed us,
fell along our bodies, making us almost see-through
as we sprayed the dust from a hundred leaves, then turned
our spray bottles on each other, laughing.
The sound of water trickling into the pond
and the wind chimes touching above us.
I knew something was up because
there were no fish in the Koi pond,
and you had removed from the high shelves your entire collection
of microscopes. You stretched out on the couch.
I went across the street
to a child's lemonade stand and brought back a paper cup
filled to the rim with lemonade and ice chips,
which you turned down.
You knew you were dying but I didn't. "Read to me," you said,
and I let my voice softly cover you. We walked across the room
to a small desk. You gave me a jewelry box, lacquered, and wooden,
with a painted wolf on it. It had been your mother's, an odd gift.
Later, we drove to the beach, got out to walk the path.
We passed an old man on a rusted-out girl's bicycle, a very old
man on a very old bike. I said kiddingly,
"That will be you in a few years."
And you said, "I'll take it."

WHAT THE DRIFTWOOD WANTS

To know the sand

before I know

the fire

COMPASS ROSE

You travel in all
directions at once
to know if the heart
can find its way
back again

AFTERWARD

This is precisely the time when [we] artists go to work.
There is no time for despair, no place for self-pity,
no need for silence, no room for fear. We speak,
we write, we do language. That is how civilization heals.

TONI MORRISON

ABOUT THE AUTHOR

KATHY EVANS is the author of three other collections of poetry: *Imagination Comes To Breakfast, As The Heart is Held,* and *Hunger and Sorrow,* which won the Small Press Poetry Prize. She has taught with California Poets in the School (now Cal Poets), at Marin County Juvenile Hall, The University of San Francisco, the College of Marin, as well as The Osher Lifelong Learning Institute. She was an artist-in-residence at the Headlands Center for the Arts, and is currently a poet-in-residence at The Benioff Children's Hospital in Oakland and San Francisco. She lives in San Rafael, California, by the library.